HIGHLY FLAMMABLE!

HIGHLY FLAMMABLE!

LIVING LIFE ON FIRE FOR GOD
A 40 DAY DEVOTIONAL

LETIA HUGHES

Let's Hug Design and Publishing
Tallahassee, Florida

Cover by Let's Hug Publishing and Design

Edited by Cynthia Portalatin Lamb

I AM HIGHLY FLAMMABLE!
Copyright © 2012 by Letia Hughes
Published by Let's Hug Publishing and Design
Tallahassee, Florida
www.letiahughes.com
 ISBN-13: 978-0615593883
All Rights reserved.

Dedication

To men and women all around the world who desire to have more of God than they had the day before. To those who are living as flames in dark places and will stop at nothing to keep their fire for God going for themselves and the people around them. Be apart of the Movement!

Special Thanks

Thank you Jesus, you are my everything. Thank you for giving me a heart to write and reach your people. I thank my family for their love, you all are a delight to my life. I want to thank my Pastors and church family for their encouragement and continuous support and my very best friends for lending a listening ear and believing in who God called me to be.

Table of Contents

Introduction

I'm so excited that you've picked up this book. God desires to see you burn with genuine love and passion for Him. Say good-bye to purposeless and passionless Christianity. You have a purpose, and it is very important. It's time for you to get on fire for God! Here are forty devotionals that can be read in any order. They are written in plain English and can be read in the morning, lunch break, before bed, whenever! I've also included lines for your thoughts.

These devotionals are meant to inspire and bring change to your life. Every instance I've written about I've gone through myself. Even in times of feeling extinguished I've read these over and over again, and I can feel my fire being ignited again.

Enjoy this book. I love you, and so does God.

Letia Hughes
a.k.a Lady Flame

Save Me!

If you were drowning and fighting for your life, you wouldn't feel ashamed or too proud to reach out and grab that lifesaver. You'd grab it and beg helplessly for the person to reel you in, feeling forever grateful to the person for saving you. There's no shame in needing to be rescued or needing to be saved.

If you haven't accepted Christ into your heart, my friend, you are drowning and you may or may not know it. Your sins – the things you do when you know you shouldn't – separate you from God (Isaiah 59:2). Don't take it personally; no one is without sin. We all need a savior.

This is why you need Jesus. God sent his son Jesus to die for you. You ask, "Why would anyone die for me?" Because He loves you! (John 3:16) No matter what you've done, and even if you were the only person who needed saving, He still would have done it for you. He doesn't want anyone to perish (2 Peter 3:9).

Another reason is that without salvation your name isn't written in the Book of Life; your final destination is the lake of fire. How could a loving God send someone to Hell? That's the thing – He's not sending people. People are choosing hell by rejecting Jesus.

You may think you're having a great time, or maybe your life sucks right now. But the truth is you will never see the goodness of God and all the wonderful things He has planned for you on this earth and in Heaven, unless you choose Jesus.

Heaven is the place you'll end up because of salvation. There are streets of gold and where people never cry. The sacrifice you must make is worth making.

It's amazing! God wants you to be in on this. Don't wait another second, for tomorrow isn't promised. Say this prayer:

Jesus, I confess I'm a sinner. I want you to be my Savior and Lord. I believe you died on the cross and rose again, so my sins could be erased. Come into my heart, and fill me with Your Spirit.

There, you have it! You're saved! Join a bible teaching church, pray every day, read your Bible daily, and watch God grow in your life.

Notes_____

_____

_____

_____

_____

_____

_____

_____

_____

_____

_____

_____

WARNING! Highly Flammable!

As believers, our lives must be highly flammable. We must be ignited with passion for God. Let's look at the characteristics of our God: it's written in Hebrews 12:29, "Our God is a consuming fire." Then Genesis 1:27 reads "We are made in the image of the Living God." Put them together, and you get spirit filled believers who are on fire for God.

Anything that is highly flammable burns easily and quickly. And fire, as we know, is not easily contained, but it spreads to anything around it. As a Christian, does your flame for God burn bright and strong? Are you a "fire starter" for the people around you? Can your friends and coworkers see and feel that warm inviting blaze?

A believer's life that is highly flammable is filled with the love of God for believers and unbelievers alike. It's focused on fulfilling the will of God for their lives. It's a life that stays seeking God, fasting and praying. A highly flammable life lives worship as a lifestyle not just lip service.

However, you may want to look out for fire extinguishers. That's your sinful nature that's at constant war with the spirit of God. Just to name a few extinguishers: sexual immorality, impurity, lustful pleasures, idolatry, sorcery, hostility, quarreling, jealousy, outbursts of anger, selfish ambition, dissension, division, envy, drunkenness, wild parties, etc. (I promise I'm quoting the Bible! Galatians 5:14) These sins are sure to snuff out your fire for God before you know it. Indulging in these will cause you to live life as a burnt-out, charred Christian. We must be consistent with our blaze to be effective. How annoying are those trick candles? One second they are going, the next they're not!

Jesus said Himself in Luke 12:49, "I have come to set the world on fire, and I wish it were already burning!" So, I challenge you to daily fan the flames! So that your passion and love for God never go out, may it be like a torch that lights the way for others. Live life submitted to God; so that you can truly say, "I am highly flammable!"

Notes_____

_____
_____
_____
_____
_____
_____
_____
_____
_____
_____
_____
_____
_____
_____
_____
_____
_____
_____
_____
_____

He's Got Love For You

The faithful love of the Lord never ends! His mercies never cease; that's Lamentations 3:22. God has love for you! I remember when I was being witnessed to, I was eighteen years old, and I thought I was having the time of my life in my senior year of high school. I grew up "churched" but never really grasped having a relationship with Jesus. The thing that really pulled me in was love. The love of God was showed to me and shared with me by a woman who gently reeled me into the love of Christ. Love penetrates the hardest of hearts and catches the attention of those who don't even realize they are looking for love.

Often times, when people aren't saved, quoting scriptures seems to bounce off their foreheads. Their hearts aren't fertile; so the Word of God doesn't take root. However, they are watching the way we live and listening to the way we talk. When witnessing, it is important to remind the person that God loves them and God wants them.

In this day in age, people of all ages and backgrounds want to be loved. People are longing to have that God shaped hole in their hearts filled. They try to fill this round hole with square pegs like drugs, sex, money, TV, relationships, food, etc.

So, I want to encourage you to let your love burn passionately for God, because His love burns passionately for you! Maybe you're the one witnessing, or you need to be witnessed to. I want you to know that God has love for you like no one else does. The Bible says that nothing can separate you from the love of God (Romans 8:38-39). Nothing you've done can change that. He wants a real relationship with you – not just a Sunday morning date.

He wants the whole thing! God's love is so resilient and so constant! It never ends and never changes. It's not based on your quota of good deeds or any other stipulations you can think of.

Don't believe the lie that you're unwanted or that nobody cares, and that your life is meaningless. Instead make a firm choice to believe that God has love for you. No matter what falls through in life, God's love is enough for you.

Notes_____

_____

_____

_____

_____

_____

_____

_____

_____

_____

_____

Let Me See Some I.D.

2 Corinthians 5:17 reads, "This means that anyone who belongs to Christ has become a new person." The old life is gone; a new life has begun!

Let me see your I.D., please. I'm sure you've been asked this question before in life. You carry your identification with you at all times. On it are your name, address and a few distinct qualities that make you – you. You know where I'm going with this – we've got a distinct spiritual identification that we carry with us because Christ, our identifier, lives in us.

People young and old, everywhere, are searching for a means to define themselves. They want to know the meaning of life... Who they are and for what purpose are they on this earth. Some would say you're defined by your money, clothes, the company you keep, or even your job. All these are just "scotch-tape" labels that can be peeled off at anytime. Let me enlighten you as to what exactly is on your Christian I.D.

First, anything you were before you accepted Jesus has been erased. You're a new person with a new life (2 Corinthians 5:17). The blood of Jesus erased all trace of the old you. Doesn't feel like it? Keep showing that I.D. to the enemy. He's got to flee every time. Why? Because you are Holy and Blameless before God (Colossians1: 12). Now under your new I.D. you can come boldly before God. You've got complete access. Right! You're under a new name!

I'm sure you can see it. It says you're a Child of God. If you're into titles, nothing beats that one. It's given to everyone that believes in Jesus (John 1:12).

Lastly, you are loved. It's so important that this is a part of your identity. You're accepted, protected and desired (1 John 4:10). It's unconditional and rather simple. He loved you before your heart started beating in your mother's womb. Now that's deep!

So let me see your I.D.! You are a new person with a new life. You are holy, blameless, a child of God, loved, and accepted. Your I.D. gives you VIP access to Jesus. So next time life challenges your identity, show them who you are by living out Christ.

Notes_____

_____

_____

_____

_____

_____

_____

_____

_____

_____

_____

_____

_____

_____

_____

_____

_____

_____

How to Be Successful

How to be successful in 30 days! How to win people! How to be a millionaire! Everyone wants success. In this time we have degrees, businesses, money, love, and family that define our state of being. While these are noticeable and wonderful accomplishments, they cannot amount to the success of pleasing God.

Pleasing God is like a fulfillment in its own. If you lost all your top accomplishments for whatever reason, would you still consider yourself a successful person? You know, even with all these things, it is impossible to please God without faith (Hebrews 11:6). If you believe what God says He'll do, you've taken your first step at being successful.

The second step is to obey God's commands for your life. What might have worked for someone else's life may not work for yours. God has a individual plan for everyone's life. Badly wanting someone else's success opens the door for covetousness and all things of that sort. Stay away! The writer says in Ecclesiastes 4:4, "Then I observed that most people are motivated to success, because they envy their neighbors. But this too is meaningless, like chasing the wind."

Sometimes you will find yourself in something that wasn't meant for you. Don't let failure enter your heart. Even the righteous falls seven times, but he rises again. Get back up, and get on the right track.

Go forward in life! Live, love and laugh. However, don't get caught up in the accolades. Get caught up in pleasing God. Be strong and very courageous. Be careful to obey all the instructions Moses gave you. Don't deviate from them; turn neither to the right nor to the left. Then you will be successful in everything you do. (Joshua 1:7).

Notes_____

_____
_____
_____
_____
_____
_____
_____
_____
_____
_____
_____
_____
_____
_____
_____
_____
_____
_____
_____
_____
_____
_____
_____

It's All Gone

A famous analogy of Christ's forgiveness is if this was court, and you were on trial for your sins, you'd be found guilty – if it had not been for Christ. Since we have Christ who took our sentence on a cross, the verdict now reads not guilty. So why are we still walking 'round here in orange jump suits, living like convicts, ashamed, and degraded.

God has forgiven you. Whatever it was, whether it be years ago or two minutes ago, if you asked Him for forgiveness, then you're forgiven. Get your heart intent on not falling again, and move forward. Proverbs 24:16 says, "The Godly Man may fall seven times, but he will get up again." Don't fall down into habitual sinning. Live life in the Spirit; so you won't fulfill the desires of the flesh.

The scriptures Colossians 2:13-14 say, "You were dead because of your sins, and because your sinful nature was not yet cut away. Then God made you alive with Christ, for He forgave all our sins. He canceled the record of the charges against us and took it away by nailing it to the cross." Everything that has been written or spoken about you, anything that's opposing you because of your sins, has been nailed to the cross. Condemnation, or what we call guilt, can't follow you anywhere if it's nailed to the cross at Calvary. Isn't that wonderful?

Shed those guilty garments and get geared up in the grace of God! You're forgiven! You've got a clean start, and God is sending a time of refreshing your way. No more guilt! It's all gone!

Notes

Christ Likes Mixed Chicks!

I know the title made some people's eyebrows go up at least one inch! But the truth of the matter is, He does! The Bride (by Bride I mean the Church) that Christ is coming back for is not one that is segregated because of race, nationality or Christian rituals. His Bride is mixed with every culture and race. So, we should pray like David did in Psalm 7:7, for God to gather the nations before Him and rule over them from on high.

A desegregated church has much to offer unbelievers and believers alike. Take the persecuted church in China. They know evangelism in a way Americans have never experienced. China's government is hostile towards Christians, and this makes it risky to pray in public, pass out Christian literature or have home Bible Studies. It's time to pray for Christians in hostile nations, because the Bride that Christ is coming back for doesn't look like you or me!

Let's look at Revelation 7:9, John is recalling what he has seen in heaven. "After this I saw a vast crowd too great to count, from every nation and tribe and people and language, standing in front of the throne and before the Lamb…" So, now that we know it's not about me, and it's not about you, let me tell you what Christ is looking for in His Bride. He's looking for a church without spot or blemish. We need not walk around with heavy make up trying to conceal the blemishes of sin and ungodliness. Christ isn't into to Botox either! No! He wants a Bride that's coming of age! A mature church that's down to earth and has her affections set on Him!

The only way we can get rid of these wrinkles and blemishes is to become Holy by the washing of the Word. Our Savior has given His life to show us how much He loves us and to present us holy and clean to Himself. So wash off the cover-up with the Word of God, and those stubborn sins will go as well.

Christ is coming soon! And like a Bride our lives should show our adoration, preparation and excitement. The Big Day is almost here! Will you be ready?

Notes_____

_____

_____

_____

_____

_____

_____

_____

_____

_____

_____

_____

_____

_____

_____

_____

_____

_____

Are We There Yet?

When did we learn that some things take a long time? When did we learn that the time it takes to do something could stretch from minutes to years? How about your first road trip as a child when you soon found out that a few hours was a long time? The words WAIT, NOT YET, HOLD OFF, and IN DUE TIME can cause that emotional lump to rise in your throat. God's got something to bring it back down.

God's timing is the best timing. It's easy for us to disagree, especially when we want something now, when it looks so good. But like a cake taken out of the oven a mere seven minutes early, the middle is undone. You can't even enjoy it, because God isn't finished with the work. Turning up the heat to rush that delectable delicacy may leave your treat dry and brittle and not as good as you imagined. Hebrews 10:36 reads, "Patient endurance is what you need now; so that you will continue to do God's will. Then you will receive all that He has promised."

A lot of scriptures in the Bible also tell us to be patient with one another. God knew we would need the reminders. 1 Corinthians 13:4 reads, "Love is patient." Be patient with those you love and those whom are strengthening your love walk. Be humble and gentle, and remember you weren't always where you are now. God was patient with you; so be patient, and make allowances for faults because of love (Ephesians 4:2). Some seasons take time to see the fruit of your patience. Continue to be patient and loving with those whom God has placed in your life.

So now, "wait," or "later," doesn't mean not ever... whether it's a few minutes or several years. Whatever God has for you is surely worth the wait. I leave you with this: Rejoice in our confident hope. Be patient in trouble, and keep on praying (Romans 12:12).

Notes_____

_____

_____

_____

_____

_____

_____

_____

_____

_____

_____

_____

_____

_____

_____

_____

_____

_____

_____

_____

_____

_____

_____

So You Wanna Hang Out Sometime?

The fellowship of believers is essential to you being on fire for God. You are a part of the body of Christ. Imagine the body being a burning campfire. Anything that separates itself from it will eventually burn out. Just like that fire, you need a church home, and you need to be able to talk to other believers in order to stay on fire for God.

The Bible says that iron sharpens iron. If other believers are not sharpening you, you will dull after being rubbed up against the frustrations of this world.

Maybe you're not into church. For whatever reason is, ask God to lead you to a place that will help you grow and be on fire for Him. The Bible says in Hebrews 10:24-25, "Let us think of ways to motivate one another to acts of love and good works. And let us not neglect our meeting together… but encourage one another." Look outside of yourself and how you feel, and think about what God wants for you.

Think of the other people who need encouragement. You have something to offer. Not only that, but you have something to do. There is so much to be done in the Kingdom of God. One person lit on fire for God is a flicker, but a group is a blaze. That's why the Bible says where two or three are gathered, in Christ name He Himself will be also. (Matthew 18:20)

No church is perfect. The truth is, you need leadership; you have something to offer, and you have something to do. The congregation is waiting. Do you want to hang out sometime?

Notes

_____

_____

_____

_____

_____

_____

_____

_____

_____

_____

_____

_____

_____

_____

_____

_____

_____

_____

_____

_____

_____

_____

_____

_____

Tie Down That Tongue

You know words are something you can never take back. Once spoken, they enter the ears of God and the hearts and minds of the people around you. The Bible says that LIFE and DEATH are in the power of the tongue – and those who love it shall eat the fruit there of (Proverbs 18:21). The words we speak have the ability to take root and bear fruit or choke the life out of the very thing that God has given us to supply our needs and bring us joy.

Let me tell you that a complaining Christian can ruin a witness so quick. How can we expect others to believe our God if we're always complaining about a situation? The children of Israel complained for a generation! They went around and around in circles for years. As a result, it took them years to enter into what God had for them. You know, it's impossible to please God without faith. (Hebrews 11:6) Are your comments full of faith and pleasing to God?

On the other hand, your words can bring life to a situation. Proverbs 10:11 says "The words of the godly are a life-giving fountain; the words of the wicked conceal violent intentions." Your words can literally be an oasis in the desert for the people around you as well as yourself. Let your words be refreshing! Proverbs 10:32 reads, "The lips of the godly speak helpful words, but the mouth of the wicked speaks perverse words." So let's distinguish ourselves! The next time you start to complain about your job, relationships, money, etc., change it up, and begin to bless God instead. I promise your day will be better. Don't let complaining taint your witness and take the joy out of living. Instead Tie Down That Tongue!

Notes_____

_____

_____

_____

_____

_____

_____

_____

_____

_____

_____

_____

_____

_____

_____

_____

_____

_____

_____

_____

_____

_____

_____

_____

Do You Love Me?
(circle yes or no)

If Jesus passed you a note that read, "Do you love me? Circle yes or no" and you circled yes, would He have nodded his head knowing you'd say yes all along? Or maybe you circled yes, and He'd say, "I wonder why I'm not told that daily? You never act like you love me." Or maybe even you'd truthfully circle no and then He'd say, "That explains why he or she doesn't act like they're in love."

Falling in love with Jesus is the fuel to your flame as a Highly Flammable Christian. Love is more than just a word. It's your worship and your life. Worship is a lifestyle. It's not just what you do or what you say – It's both.

Jesus says that to love God is to obey His commands (1 John 5:3). When you fall in love with someone, you love doing what pleases them. You love to make them smile and laugh. The same is with God. You obey Him, because it makes Him happy. It fills your own heart with joy and adoration as well.

Love is not only what you do; it's what you say. If you only heard "I love you" once from someone, but they also did nice things for you, you'd consider that person a friend, right? But Jesus is calling you to more than friendship. He's calling you to marriage. Yes, whether you are male or female, you're engaged to Christ. So then act like it, and show Jesus some intimate love. He is so loveable. It's easy once you get started. Try I love you! I glorify you; I magnify you; you amaze me!

The book of Psalms is full of worship. Psalms 9:12 reads, "I will praise you, O Lord, with all my heart. I will tell of all your wonders. I will be glad and rejoice in you; I will sing praises to your name, O most high." Live out your love for God!

Notes_____

_____

_____

_____

_____

_____

_____

_____

_____

_____

_____

_____

_____

_____

_____

_____

_____

_____

_____

_____

_____

_____

_____

Forgive Them

"I just can't forgive them, not after what they did!" There always seems to be a good reason for unforgiveness. And I know that whatever "They" did had an enormous impact on your life thus far. But now the choice is up to you as to whether or not you will be a great impact in the Kingdom of God or will unforgiveness be a catastrophic impact in your own life.

Let's talk about what forgiveness isn't. It isn't saying that what the other person did is right. It doesn't mean that you put yourself in the same environment for it to happen again. What forgiveness means is releasing that person; so you can receive God's forgiveness. It unlocks the cell you've placed yourself in, and it allows you to come out and live your life.

If you forgive people, your Father in heaven will forgive you. If you don't forgive, then you won't be forgiven (Matthew 6:14-15). This is because you're passing judgment on people. There is only one just judge, and that's God! You must forgive; so that you can receive your own forgiveness.

Unforgiveness is like a sickness that hardens your heart, your will and your thought life. Keep holding on to it, and you'll be hardened on the outside as well. Unforgiveness can take years off your life. You want to know why? Because you stay stagnate, and life itself is going on without you. Think of the joy you could have, the relationships you could be enjoying, if only you could let that person and the events go.

How? It's a choice. Yep. It means saying it and acting like it and believing it. Allow God in your heart; He knows what happened, and He cares but it's for you to let it go. Bare with each other and forgive whatever grievances you may have against one another. Forgive as the Lord forgave you (Colossians 3:13).

Notes_____

_____

_____

_____

_____

_____

_____

_____

_____

_____

_____

_____

_____

_____

_____

_____

_____

_____

_____

_____

_____

_____

Giving To God

When we as humans give gifts to others, we feel great about what we're doing. We often desire for them to open it as soon as possible; so we can see their expression of joy. Giving is great! Giving to God is even greater!

Some may ask, "What does God need with my money?" The real question is this, "What do you need with God's money?" Everything on the Earth belongs to Him. He's only asking for 10% of it back. If we can give good gifts to our loved ones, can we give a good gift to God without questioning His motives? Malachi 3 speaks of tithing. Not tithing is considered robbing God, but when you do tithe, God will provide for your needs. Malachi 3:10 says, "Try it! Put me to the test." Forget about everything negative you've heard about tithes and offerings, and believe God's word.

Of equal importance is giving of your gifts or talent. This seems so evident, but people often time give their gifts to themselves. Friend, you have a gift that God has given you. Maybe it's preaching, serving or even cleaning or accounting. Whatever it is, be sure not to use it for your own personal gain. Be sure to develop it, practice it and protect it.

Always remember to give God the glory. Matthew 25:14 tells the parable of the three servants that were given talents. Two of those invested and labored over their talents. The one with one talent buried it.

In the end the servant with one had his talent taken away, because he did nothing with it. Be sure to be like the other two and invest ALL the talents keeping none for yourself.

Give back to God in money and in gifts. You're sowing seeds that will cause growth in you and your family.

Notes_____

_____

_____

_____

_____

_____

_____

_____

_____

_____

_____

_____

_____

_____

_____

_____

_____

_____

_____

_____

_____

_____

The Pot Calling The Potter Whack

Isaiah 29:16 reads like this, "How foolish can you be? He is the Potter, and he is certainly greater than you, the clay! Should the created thing say of the one who made it, 'He didn't make me?' Does a jar ever say, "The potter who made me is stupid"?"

God why am I like this? God when? God where? God why not? I have no problem with asking God questions, but when your questions turn into you challenging God's plan for your life, it's time to get back on that wheel. When a potter picks up a piece of clay, the clay sits on the potter's wheel being spun and smoothed and shaped until it reaches the potter's desire. So are we in the hands of our Father.

When a songwriter writes to a beat, the beat has no choice as to whether it's a soulful love song or a child's lullaby. When a painter paints on a canvas, the canvas has no choice as to whether it will be splashed with random colors or a beautiful landscape. Though we have no choice in our purpose (other than to follow it or not), I want you to know we have peace, because our creator never makes mistakes.

Unlike any random painter and canvas, we have this assurance we are God's masterpiece! He has created us anew in Christ Jesus; so we can do the good things He planned for us long ago (Ephesians 2:10). Friend, no matter your purpose, God's plans for you are good, full of hope and a future (Jeremiah 29:11).

God has a unique frame that your life fit's into. His plans are to set you front-and-center for His glory. Perhaps your life will be on view at your school, at your job, at your church, or even in your circle of friends. Regular wall art doesn't get this kind of treatment. You're a masterpiece!

Don't let the trials of this life make you think that you're anything less. We serve a good God that loves us. So, then why is the pot calling the potter whack? Why are we shaking our heads at God as if he doesn't have the faintest idea as to what He's doing? Do you disagree with how your life is going now? Trust you're a priceless work of art, and that the God who made you has an awesome purpose for you. Despite what you're dealing with or going through now, whether you think you're overweight or unskilled, whether you think you're too shy or not smart enough... Be who God called you to be! Highly Flammable!

Notes_____

_____

_____

_____

_____

_____

_____

_____

_____

_____

A Piece of God

Break me off a piece of God! Everyone needs a piece of God. He is giving out pieces of Himself free of charge, and the amount is endless!

Colossian 3:16 reads, "Let the peace of Christ rule in your hearts, since as members of one body you were called to Christ." Yes, it's true the peace of God can rule your life. What an awesome feat that peace can be in charge of your actions, your emotions and your heart.

I know you wonder how you could have peace, despite what's going on. Listen friend, the Bible says in 1 John 4:15, "All who confess that Jesus is the Son of God have God living in them, and they live in God."

So, now you know it's true! You really do have a piece of God inside you. It's up to you as to whether it's large or small; ask for peace and you shall receive. Psalm 29:11 reads, "The Lord blesses His people with peace."

Anything but God's peace is a false peace. You won't find peace trying to take pleasure in other things. Though they may feel like peace, they will leave you dissatisfied after a while. Consider yourself starving, and you just keep eating rice cakes! Instead, the Father has gifted you with a feast laid out for you. Dig in! Break off a piece of God's peace. Meditate on Jesus, and He will fill you up.

Notes

Burnt To A Crisp

If you've got a lot on your plate, you should be cautious of burning out for Christ. If you're not fueled up, you'll be burnt out. This is a result of too much ministry and not enough relationship. A little offense is all it takes for you to reevaluate why you hang around Christians at all. Instead of being on fire for God, you'll be a burnt-to-a-crisp Christian.

Without the relationship, ministry is just deeds. Good deeds won't get you into heaven. You have to have the relationship to match. Good deeds will make you feel good, and will make others around you feel good as well. But if you don't have the inspiration that starts with God, whenever hard times come you'll get burnt out. Everything you do – do as though you're doing it for God. (Colossians 3:23)

Offense! Don't allow offense to fence you in. It's like using a spray bottle on a candle. If water saturates the wick, the fire will go out. A root of bitterness will grow in your ministry. And that pertains to that platform ministry and the marketplace ministry. I want to encourage you to work at living in peace with everyone. Look out for others; so that know one will miss the grace of God. Bitterness is trouble for you and corrupts everyone around you (Hebrews12:14-15).

If this sounds like you; if you feel like your edges are already starting to singe, there's hope for you. Pray and rest in God. He gives rest to the weary and joy to the sorrowing (Jeremiah 31:25). He'll chip away the char to reveal a new you!

Notes

Faithful

The first commandment given to Moses was to not have any god before God. Back in those days the children of Israel had just come out of an idol saturated country. God wanted to make sure that they knew He was to remain the first and only God in their lives. Some religions today still practice the worship of idols. And as Christians sometimes we place other things or people before God making them idols.

One thing is to remain clear and true – There is only one living God (Jeremiah 10:10). And that's our God! Any other god is dead and an inanimate object made by the hands of man. They can't see or speak or hear. Why consult mediums, spirits, physics, or horoscopes? Just ask God, Himself; He created the stars! (Isaiah 8:19) Be faithful in your relationship with God by laying down all your other sources and making God your one and only. Don't mix religions. Adding anything else to Christ is like adding bitter water to clean water.

So, you don't have any man-made object in your heart stealing love from God? Anything you love a little bit more than God, anything that has any competition with your relationship with God, is an idol. Television, Internet, your job, your kids, even that special someone can be an idol. Be faithful in your relationship with God. The book of revelation shares Jesus' heart as He's says, "But I have the complaint against you. You don't love me or each other as you did at first" (Revelation 2:4). In this relationship, consistency is the key!

The Bible is filled with scriptures about God's faithfulness. Will the book that tells your story be filled with your faithfulness too?

Notes_____

_____

_____

_____

_____

_____

_____

_____

_____

_____

_____

_____

_____

_____

_____

_____

_____

_____

_____

_____

_____

_____

_____

_____

_____

Just Say No!

If you want to be nothing left but a pile of ashes, instead of a blazing fire for God, just say yes to temptation. Of course even a righteous man falls, but he gets back up! He doesn't roll all around on the ground. Habitually falling into sin and rolling in it, is like stop, drop and roll. FIRE OUT.

Sin strains our relationship with God. You may not feel the strain at first. But believe me, it's there. If you keep on, it will grow until your relationship with God is dangling by a thread. God's presence won't be able to fuel your fire any longer. It'll be a fighting flicker as opposed to a blowtorch.

Now hear this: God is powerful and mighty to save! And though it may seem like that thing has you stuck and won't let go, do your part, and God will always do His.

Your part: Pray. Resist. Stay Away. Whatever your issue is, stay prayed up concerning it every day. Don't be ashamed. Look up scriptures that match your situation. Secondly, resist the Devil, and he will flee from you (James 4:7). This doesn't mean resist once, and say it didn't work. Resist all day, every day and every time. Last but not least, stay away from those things that tempt you to sin, those things in life that always draw you into actions that make you feel ashamed and guilty.

God's Part: He is your help. He's the very thing you need to say no. Hebrews 2:18 says, "Because He himself suffered when he was being tempted, He is able to help those who are being tempted." Yes, even Jesus was tempted but without sin (Hebrews 4:15). He knows what you need, and if you want to be free with His help it can be done!

Like I said earlier, even the righteous fall. In the event you do fall, get back up quickly, repent and keep going!

Notes

_____

_____

_____

_____

_____

_____

_____

_____

_____

_____

_____

_____

_____

_____

_____

_____

_____

_____

_____

Fly High!

You've been riding a four-wheeler around town, but recently you've been invited to a plush business rendezvous across the country. I doubt you're going to be putting that low rider on the road. The wear and tear of the drive will probably have your ride shakin' and bakin' by the time you reach the city limits. You're going to need to take flight!

Life's terrain is sure to break you down, the bumpy roads of disappointment, the mountains of bills, and let's not forget the cracks in the road from snappy remarks from friends, family and co-workers. If you want to get anywhere, and in a timely fashion, you're going to have to fly over that environment.

Ephesians 2:6 explains that we are dead to fleshy reactions. By the flesh, I mean snobby retorts and ungodly comebacks and the need to make sure you have the last word.

You see, when we fly over those situations, we never feel those "bumps." The Bible says that those who trust in the Lord will find new strength. They will soar high on wings like eagles (Isaiah 40:31). If we put our trust in the Lord, we will be able to fly like eagles. Don't sap your strength with retaliation. You'll find yourself biking up mountains again. It also goes on to say, "That they will walk and not faint and run and not be weary." Trust in God to vindicate you, instead of doing it yourself.

Remember, you're an eagle. You're created to soar over dangerous traps. In fact, you can look down and enjoy the view. So, start walking, break into a run and take off! Happy travels!

Notes

Murder She Spoke

"I'll pray for you!" "Don't say anything but…" How many times have these words been spoken? How many times have ears been lent to hear juicy conversation? It was murder that was spoken over your sisters or brothers in Christ.

Leviticus 19:6 states "Do not spread slanderous gossip among your people. Do not stand idly by when your neighbor's life is threatened. I am the LORD." While it may not be fatal in the natural, words hurt. They take the life out of that person's integrity – and yours. Question. Why do you think at the end of that scripture God felt that He needed to remind us that He is the Lord? If you're gossiping out of anger and hurt, you'll get no vindication, because vengeance is the Lord's. See, most times gossip is meant to hurt and destroy a person's character, because they hurt you or because of jealousy. If you know compromising info on a not-so-favorite friend, take the Godly route, and pray them out.

It doesn't matter if it's the truth! Or even if you don't necessarily think it's mean! Or if people will hear it anyway. Psalm 34:13 says, keep your tongue from evil and your lips from speaking lies. God wouldn't ask you to do something that, the Holy Spirit couldn't help you with. Maybe you're the gossiper with the down low on everyone. Maybe you just blurt it out, or maybe you're just angry. Either way, the Lord desires to help you. He can change your life; so that you are now the person who can speak highly of anyone when everyone else is bringing him or her down.

Perhaps you're the person who is listening and not saying much, because you're friends with the gossiper. You don't want to jeopardize the friendship or seem, "too holy." Well, I've got news for you. God says, "be Holy for I am I holy," (I Peter 1:15-16). Speak up, change the subject, and pray for your friend. May the Lord grant you boldness as you speak life!

Notes

Power up!

One thing I love about the Lord – and I mean it always get's me fired up! It's His power! We are dusty dumplings compared to the might of Jesus! When Christ rose from the dead, He rose with all power! And Christians have the same power working in them that raised Christ from the dead (Romans 8:11).

Anything that's powerless is purposeless. Yank any household appliance from the socket and you've got a giant paperweight. Perhaps you can put your junk mail on top! Friend, that's not the life God has called you to! You are highly flammable and powerful, and God wants to use you!

Ephesians 3:20 reads, "Now all glory to God, who is able, through his mighty power at work within us, to accomplish infinitely more than we might ask or think." Perhaps you think you're just a regular person; maybe you even see yourself as weak. But God gives power to the weak and strength to the powerless (Isaiah 40:29).

You are saved, and that's what's important, but the adventure doesn't stop there.   With God's power working through you, there is power to bring people to Christ (Acts 1:8), power to heal (James 5:14), and power to resist the devil and his devices (Luke 10:19).

Now you know you have power, and you know whose power is working through you. But how do you power up? Remember that appliance? Exactly! You stay plugged in to God.

This power is not for recreation; it is for God's glory. And in order to operate, you must stay close to God, walk in Holiness and stay humble. Live through the power of God, and live out your purpose.

Notes

Ask For Directions

You just arrived in a brand new city. You've got places to go, people to see and things to do! Will you ride around the hotel in a circle, or will you stop and ask for directions so you can reach your destination timely? This is day to day life! Your walk with God is brand new every day. Don't put on unneeded mileage turning down dead end streets or riding around in circles.

If God is the GPS for your life, trust Him – He's got the satellite view! He can see oncoming traffic and guide you away from accidents. Unlike technology, He's always up to date, never needs an upgrade. All you have to do is ask. Trust in the Lord with all your heart, and lean not on your own understanding, and He will make your path straight (Proverb 3:5-6).

God has a plan. It involves you going here, there and stopping to gas up. Don't trust your gut! Trust God. Never be too in a hurry, thinking you don't have enough time to hear from God. Haste makes waste. If you wait and listen, you'll hear what the directions are. Your own ears will hear him. Right behind you a voice will say, "This is the way you should go, whether to the right or to the left." (Isaiah 30:21).

Now you've got directions – follow them. Don't slam it into drive when God just told you to reverse!

Don't spin your wheels leaving God in the dust calling out, "I know a shorter, better, smoother way!" It may start off smooth, but that road's going to crumble, your tires are going to lose their traction, and your check-engine light is going to come on with smoke coughing out the muffler. God's way is the best way.

He says "I will instruct you and teach you in the way you should go. I will counsel you and watch over you" (Psalm 32:8). He's got the best view and the best understanding. He's got the best plan and everything you need to get to your destination.

Notes_____

_____
_____
_____
_____
_____
_____
_____
_____
_____
_____
_____
_____
_____
_____
_____
_____
_____
_____

You Make Me So Angry!

Some of us get angry every day. Some of us not often at all. But one thing you want to know, regardless, is how to stay in right standing with God. When you're angry, you often won't have the response that pleases God unless you've submitted it to God. And by the way, I'm not talking about righteous anger. I'm talking about how you feel when you're about to go off!

Regardless of whether your anger is right or wrong, the first step is self-control. That means know how to walk away and pray. It may take a serious humbling experience, but it's the safest way. Proverbs 25:28 reads, "A person without self-control is like a city with broken down walls." That means anything can come out your mouth, and words spoken can get in and activate offense making you unprotected. You must maintain self-control! After you have breathed for a minute and heard from God, then you'll know whether it was a minor offense or something you should approach the person about.

Jesus said, if you hold anger in your heart against someone, it's like being a murderer (Matthew 5:21-22). We all have done wrong, and though you probably haven't done what the person has done or you haven't set up a person like you were set up, you've still made someone angry.

Take a second to remember that you need God's forgiveness, and grant it to that person. Let it go, and move on.

It may mean continuing the relationship or letting it go. It's all up to God, just remember a fool is quick tempered, but a wise person stays calm when insulted (Proverbs 12:16).

Notes

_____

_____

_____

_____

_____

_____

_____

_____

_____

_____

_____

_____

_____

_____

_____

_____

_____

_____

_____

_____

_____

Name it!

Name: word by which a person is pointed out. What's in a name? Your name is what sets you aside from the rest. It's so important that you know what God calls you, and that he has called you specifically by name. God has an individual call on your life. It may or may not be for the nations; it may or may not be the marketplace, but it's specifically for you.

Almost everyone who has gone to school has been called names. Maybe they weren't completely mean. Perhaps they called you "average student" or branded you with at least "you're smart." Where am I going with this? You've got to respond to what God calls you – not what anyone else says.

You see, all through the Old and New Testament God is going around changing peoples names. Abraham, Sarah, Paul, Jacob… just to name a few. God's word never returns back to Him without accomplishing its purpose (Isaiah 55:11). So, whatever God has called you to do is specific, and that calling is only for you.

We have happy memories of the Godly, but the name of a wicked person rots away (Proverbs 10:7). Your name is attached to how people recall you. Does your name ring with godliness? Listen, I don't care what anybody has called you. If it doesn't line up with God's word, then discard it. It can no longer define you nor set you apart from what God has for you.

You are not another nameless face in the crowd. God can't stop thinking about you. He's got your name tattooed on His hand (Isaiah 49:16). Yes! Little known secret: God has tattoos! (Not saying you should though. ☺)

God has called you – yes, YOU, by name from the womb. Wow! So even before your parents thought of your name, God already knew you. God has a specific, unique assignment for *Your Name Here*. And no one can fill the spot in His heart but you!

Notes_____

_____
_____
_____
_____
_____
_____
_____
_____
_____
_____
_____
_____
_____
_____
_____
_____
_____
_____
_____

How Low Can You Go?

If our walk with God is like the game limbo, how low would we go? By that I mean, how humble can you be? Getting low is the only way to get higher with God. He exalts the humble and loves the proud. When the bar is lowered, can you hang in there? Or will you fall out?

You know, our savior Christ was the most humble man to walk this earth. He is King of everything, yet He became a man and suffered a criminal's death to save the entire Earth, knowing some would never accept Him. He went to the death without a complaint. He knew He was King, and yet He came to serve. Amazing!

If you'll recall, David was chased for years by Saul. David had many opportunities to overthrow Saul, but he never did. He waited on God and humbled himself. Then God exalted him as king, even though he was anointed king years before.

Instead of taking the high road that is filled with your own wisdom, take the low road, and let others sing your praises (Proverbs 27:2). Like limbo, getting down low isn't easy.
And you can be sure that the road for David and Jesus wasn't a comfortable one, but God helped them through. The Lord will sustain the humble but cast the wicked to the ground (Psalm 147:6).

So friends, humble yourselves under the hand of God. His hand is shelter for you, and He will lift you in due time.

Notes

Let's Talk It Over

Prayer changes everything; it's like a weapon in war or a nice warm blanket on a winter day. It's like medicine when you're sick, and it's like a good laugh on a not so good day. Prayer is talking to God.

If you want to know what God wants you to do, pray about it (Jeremiah 33:3). It's your direct line of communication to God. When you open your mouth, His ears are already open. We can confidently talk to God who, by the way, is very interested in what you have to say. If we ask anything according to His will, He hears us (1 John 5:14).

Talk to God, whisper to Him, cry out to Him as often as you can use your lips. The Bible says that when you call on God, and you're praising and confessing your sin, He will listen (Psalm 66:16-20). God loves to communicate with you, because He loves you.

Well, what should you pray about then? Pray about everything. Listen, your prayers do not have to be loud, or drawn out or intellectual. God knows what's on your heart, but it matters to Him that you convey it. Pray in the Spirit (By God's Spirit) on all occasions with all kinds of prayers and requests. Stay alert, and be persistent in your prayers for all believers everywhere (Ephesians 6:18).

It was the prayers of great people that changed nations. Isaiah, Moses and even Jesus, being closer to God than anyone else, often took time out for prayer. Got something on your heart? Talk it over with God.

Notes

Finding Joy

It's easy to find things to be happy with on a good day. On a bad day, maybe not so much. Maybe you'll go old school and stomp and praise God for shoes on yo' feet and the clothes on yo' back! But maybe you don't have all those things. What if you do now, but because of whatever situation you lost your possessions. Where would you find your joy?

One day Jesus' disciples came bouncing up to Him clicking their heels. They were rejoicing, because they were able to cast out demons and pray with power. Jesus quickly reminded them to rejoice, because their name is written in the book of life instead (Luke 10:20).

Friend, there is joy in Salvation. There is joy in God's unchanging love and grace. The Bible says the things that are seen are temporary, but the things that are unseen are eternal. You may be able to reach out and touch those tangible things that bring you happiness. And that's great! But circumstances can cause those things to lose their glimmer. Though the love of Jesus, His grace and His mercy are things you won't be able to touch. They are always there, even when everything else seems chaotic. He loves forever! Happiness is fleeting, but joy is eternal!

Friend, if you have accepted Jesus as your Lord and Savior, then you have salvation and eternal life. Rejoice! Ask the Lord to restore the joy of your salvation   (Psalm 51:12). Shout with Joy to the Lord! And sing a new song as you think on Jesus; He is guaranteed to make you smile. Always be full of joy in the Lord. I say it again, rejoice! (Philippians 4:4)

Notes

FUNKADELIC

Sometimes, when my friends are having a bad day, they often say they are in a 'funk." You know, that feeling that you have of indifference. Not really happy, not really mad, borderline sad? Of course you do! I want to talk to you about turning that funky attitude back into one that's filled with spunk.

You're bound to have moody days. Every once in a while you may wake up on the wrong side of the bed. Perhaps you're tired of your job or the people around you. Whatever the reason, your attitude can make your day better.

First things first, get to God! He knows exactly what you need: a hug, a smile, laughter. He desires to help you with your attitude. Your attitude is reflected by what's happening in your spirit. You cannot have a joyous spirit with a funky attitude. Psalm 73:26 reads, "My health may fail, and my spirit may grow weak, but God remains the strength of my heart; he is mine forever." Shake yourself! God is the strength of your heart. Remembering, God's uncompromising love for you is sure to make your day better.

That is why we never give up. Though our bodies are dying, our spirits are being renewed daily (2 Corinthians 4:16). Let me clue you in on a little secret. Maybe you didn't receive the newness this morning, but at any part of the day you can put on that newness. A fresh start can happen. Now all you have to do is make up your mind.

Speaking of minds. How you feel has a lot to do with what's on your mind. Try thinking some thoughts that are true, honorable, right, pure, lovely, admirable, excellent, and worthy of praise (Philippians 4:8). Remember, the truth about who God says you are and what you are called to do.

So, change out of that funky attitude! Get to God! He'll renew your spirit and change your thoughts. Ephesians 4:23-24 reads, "Instead, let the Spirit renew your thoughts and attitudes. Put on your new nature, created to be like God – truly righteous and holy." Oh yes, the FUNK went out with the 60's!

Notes_____

_____
_____
_____
_____
_____
_____
_____
_____
_____
_____
_____
_____
_____
_____
_____
_____
_____
_____

All By Ourselves

Single. Little to no friends. Family lives in another state. You're in a room full of people talking and laughing, but you still feel so alone. Feelings can get the best of you. Especially when you're by yourself, and God feels so far away. Loneliness is a negative feeling, but it doesn't have to be your reality.

The Bible encourages Godly relationships, and you need to be connected to other believers. But let's face it, sometimes there's nobody to go to the movies with. And that's fine! You're never alone. God may feel far, but He isn't! God said in his word, "He'll never leave your or forsake you" (Hebrews 13:5).

Now, myself turns into ourselves! Jesus is that friend that the Bible talks about. He sticks closer than a brother (Proverbs18: 24). He desires your companionship and to hear about your day. He wants to hear about the things that made you upset with your kids, your friends, your job, and whatever else. God is who He says He is. One of His great names is Emmanuel – God is with us.

We are caught up in a world where everything is tangible, and you can actually see it. If there isn't someone in the car with us, we think it's obvious that we're alone. We must change our mindset to believe that God is with us. He hears us, and He loves us (Psalm 145:18). The Lord is near to all who call on Him (Micah 7:7). The scripture reads, in Psalm 149:4, "Therefore I will look to the Lord; I will wait for the God of my salvation; My God will hear me. For the Lord delights in His people; He crowns the humble with victory."

So, you see, you don't have to be sad and lonely. Take this time to befriend God. Resist the urge to fill the void with things and people that will never satisfy. With God you're never alone!

Notes_____

_____
_____
_____
_____
_____
_____
_____
_____
_____
_____
_____
_____
_____
_____
_____
_____
_____
_____
_____
_____
_____
_____

Shame Shame Go Away

Everyone makes mistakes or wrong decisions. Some have much worse consequences than others. The important thing is not to compare yourself to other people. When a person's eyes are opened to their sin, they become aware of their shortcomings, and they often feel ashamed. Shame stops you from being the real you.

Shame is all in the mind, but people act like it's a veil over their faces. Whatever happened is in the past. If you've repented, then God has forgiven you. God knows your past, but He sees your future. Don't ever let anyone, not even yourself, make you feel ashamed, and stand on that. Isaiah 50:7 says, "Because the sovereign Lord helps me, I will not be disgraced like a stone, determined to do His will, and I know I will not be put to shame." Know who you live for now, and get stuck on that belief.

No doubt, sin is filthy no matter what the sin. However, God Himself is willing to help with this sinful scandal. He says, "Come now, let's settle this." Says the Lord. "Though your sins are like scarlet, I will make them as white as snow though; they are red like crimson, I will make them as white as wool." (Isaiah 1:18) Isn't that exciting? Even though you've got a shameful lawsuit against you, Christ died on the cross so that your shame could be settled.

Don't allow your shame or your past to keep you from Christ. Remain in fellowship with Him; so that when He returns, you will be full of courage and not shrink back from Him in shame (1 John 2:28).

Notes

Swing My Way

Delight yourself in the Lord and He will give you the desires of your heart (Psalm 37:4). We swing far and wide on this scripture like a kid on a tire swing hoping to get what we desire from God. Now mind you, I'm not saying God's word isn't true at all. All I'm saying is, you can't box God into getting what you desire from Him.

I can't tell you how many times God has told me to wait when I thought things were going to swing my way. I shouted and pouted and cried only at the last second to have things to go my way. God was allowing me to see my lack of trust in Him for that area in my life. And sometimes, well, things didn't swing my way. Often times, I had to do something I didn't want to do. I found what I didn't want to do was for my benefit. I may not have loved it, but I love the character it brought out of me.

I want you to know, regardless of your circumstance, no matter which scenario you fit into, God's way is the best way. Let's look at King Jesus, in the garden of Gethsemane. Matthew 26:38 says, he was overwhelmed with sorrow! Yet in verse 39, He's asking, is there a way I won't have to do this? Yet not my way, but your way... Jesus Himself wanted God's way above His own, though He knew it would be painful! He knew it was the best way. Sounds like an oxymoron, right?

Philippians 1:29 reads, "For you have been given not only the privilege of suffering for Him." Whoa! Who saw that coming? So, my friend will you take up your cross on this day? Let your love for God totally eclipse what's trying to overtake you. Delight yourself in the Lord regardless of what you want or desire or whether or not things swing your way.

Notes_____

_____
_____
_____
_____
_____
_____
_____
_____
_____
_____
_____
_____
_____
_____
_____
_____
_____
_____
_____
_____

I'm Not Scared of You!

Fear. Some of us pay ten dollars to be scared silly at a movie theatre. While some of us are praying for God to deliver us from our greatest fears – we'd pay anything to be free. Maybe your fear is heights, being alone, the past, present, or future. Whatever it is, you don't have to be afraid any longer.

Fear is a bully. It pushes you around. You're afraid to turn corners in life for fear of what may happen. You may be scared of being turned upside down and having everything that's precious to you slip out of your pockets.

But unlike the kid that's bullied, you've got a whole army to fight for you. You've got Jesus! He's mighty, powerful and nobody messes with His people! David says in Psalm 27:1-3, "The Lord is my light and my salvation – so why should I be afraid? The Lord is my fortress, protecting me from danger – so why should I tremble? When evil people come to devour me, they will stumble and fall. Though a mighty army surrounds me, my heart will not be afraid. Even if I am attacked, I will remain confident."

There's a man that fought both lion and giant. He had good reason to cower! But instead, he remembered who God is. He's a fortress that protects from danger and people. David also says even when it looks like he won't win, he will still trust in God. Another investing tidbit is verse 3 when he says "even if I am attacked." Now these, "Attacks," will come, but be confident in God – you have no reason to fear.

Remember God loves you, even when it seems the enemy is assaulting you everywhere you turn. I like the scripture that says, "God has not given us the spirit of fear but of power, love and a sound mind" (2 Timothy 1:7 KJV). Speak out loud who God is, and live out all God has given you!

Notes_____

_____

_____

_____

_____

_____

_____

_____

_____

_____

_____

_____

_____

_____

_____

_____

_____

_____

_____

_____

_____

_____

Just A Little Closer

The word personal, as it pertains to our personal relationship with God, doesn't mean we shouldn't share it with others. It only means that your relationship with God is unique and something you must invest in personally.

You may be on fire for God and involved in ministry, or maybe you and Jesus are just on a first name basis, and you speak only in passing. You can always come a little closer. You can always get to know God better.

How then can you get to know God better? Like any other person, you spend time with them. God himself has invited you closer to His son Jesus (1 Corinthians 1:9).

Spend time with God in your thoughts. On your job, while you are hard at work, meditating on God makes you work day lighter (Psalm 145:5). Talk to God. Prayer is not as formal as you think. Go ahead, He's asking for you to come and talk with Him (Psalm 27:8).

If you want to be closer to someone, you tell him or her you love them and you spend time with them. Love creates a bond not easily broken. Focus on loving God because of who He is, not just for what He can do. Psalm 100:2 says, "Worship the Lord with gladness."

So you see, God wants to be closer to you. Despite everything you've done and will do, He still wants to be closer to you. He's already taken the step; now it's your turn. Come close to God, and He'll come even closer to you.

Notes

Thanks A Lot

I can't begin to stress the importance of a grateful heart. There isn't a person on this earth that isn't turned off by an ungrateful heart. When someone blesses you, walking away without saying thank you is considered rude. It will make you want to recant whatever kind word or deed you just did. Thankfully, God isn't like man. And that is one reason we should tell God thanks.

All over the Bible, there are accounts of people giving thanks to God from the Old Testament to the New. Don't hold back your gratefulness. God loves to hear your praises! Sing praises to God, and do not be silent (Psalm 30:11-12). Whenever you start to give thanks out loud to God, ticking off all the wonderful works He's done makes the situations in your life that are shaky more stable. You're reminded of His faithfulness. Instead of a "to do list," it's an "already done list!"

God loves to receive your thanks. And why should you thank Him? Because He's good! Jesus' death and resurrection are just a start. And when you think of all His wonderful deeds in your life, a passing nod is not enough. So then tell the Lord thank ya! Praise Him with shouts of joy! Praise Him with dancing, music, poetry, and whatever you do – do it for God.

He loves you, and He loves your thankfulness so much (Psalm 149:4). For He delights in you; praise pleases Him, and it builds you. Tell God thank ya!

Notes

Do you trust me?

Remember that part in all the Epic films? The guy and the girl are in danger, and then the guy reaches his hand out to the girl and says, "Do you trust me?" The girl nods yes, taking his hand, and they jump from a burning building to land safely somewhere. It's classic! And so God is asking you the same question. He's reaching out his hand asking you, "Do you trust me?"

You know, if anybody's trustworthy, it's God. Thousands of years of promises in His word, and He's never broken one. He's not like man; so He won't lie to you. But just don't take my word for it. Get to know Him. Trust is built on a person's character, and how well you know they'll respond. Once you know a person, you'll know whether to believe them or not. God's word is true, and we can trust everything He does (Psalm 33:4).

Trust is essential in this day and age. If you don't trust in God, you will trust in something. And that something may hold out for a little, but it cannot endure the weight of man's worries. It will fail you. Jesus confidently tells us to put our trust in Him and not to let our heart be troubled (John 14:1). It's such relief that we can cast all our concerns on God!

God's very nature is to love and care about you. Don't depend on your own understanding of life; trust in the Lord with all your heart (Proverbs 3:5). He won't let you down.

Notes

Taking the Witness Stand

You've been subpoenaed. It's mandatory, and there's no way you can get out of your testimony. Watching and listening is a full courtroom waiting to hear your life's testimony.

It's true. Check out Acts 1:8, But you will receive power when the Holy Spirit has come upon you, and you will be my witness in the whole world (paraphrased).

In order to be a credible witness for Christ, you'll want to be reliable, truthful and have a testimony of faith.

It's all spelled out in Proverbs: a false witness will be cut off, but a credible witness will be allowed to speak (Proverbs 21:28). Then in Proverbs 14:25, "A truthful witness saves lives." So, then tell the truth about God by the way you speak and the way you live; so that others might be saved.

The easiest part is saying how good God is. It's easy to say God loves you. But when you take the stand in life's courtroom, people won't only be listening to your words – they'll be looking at your life.

When you take the stand, remember to love. This is how people will know that your testimony is credible. Jesus said love others like He loved, unconditionally and consistently.

Bottom line is this. Don't be a false alarm. Really be on fire for Christ, because of your life and what you speak about God. Not a cloud of smoke that dissipates with the wind. Speak a true testimony that will leave the jury with real conviction.

Notes

Just Do It

Jesus says, "If you love me, you'll obey my commandments (John 14:15). What? Do you mean loving God isn't just great worship music and sincere prayers? It's not just Sunday morning services? Nope! It includes obedience. Tough pill to swallow? No, you can't break it in half. You just have to do it.

It's easy to obey new and exciting instructions. But the instructions that are not on top of your priority list can leave you with a sour look on your face. So you decide to do something else. You think to yourself, "I know what will really get the job done, what will really make God happy." Hold it right There! You're coming down with a case of arrogance. Take this obedience with a tall glass of humility! The prophet Samuel in the Old Testament said, "Obedience is better than sacrifice" (1 Samuel 15:22). What does this mean to us now? I'll tell you; it means do the will of your father in heaven and not your own. God knows exactly what He wants from you. When He gives you instructions, take it – it's good for you.

So, you ask, what if it isn't good? I ask you this – Isn't God good? Great things happen when you obey. Things are not so great when you don't obey, even if it seems like you're flying high. Proverbs 29:18 reads, "When people do not accept divine guidance, they run wild. But whoever obeys the law is joyful." Yes, there is joy in doing even the things you don't want to do, because you are pleasing your Father in heaven.

Don't make your own way out, when God has given you the right way out. Keep your focus on God, and just do it!

Notes_____

_____

_____

_____

_____

_____

_____

_____

_____

_____

_____

_____

_____

_____

_____

_____

_____

_____

_____

_____

_____

_____

_____

You're Getting Off My Last Nerve!

Aggravation. Irritation. It seems that as soon as you begin to burn for God here comes aggravation using a pogo stick to ride your nerves. If you can imagine trying to sleep, and someone is right by your ear with cymbals… whenever you start to drift off… CRASH! How irritating is that? Even more so, how distracting from your purpose, sleep.

No matter how much you love God, there will always be things that irritate you. You're human! But it's a choice that we have to make to not allow distractions to detour us. See, aggravation comes to take your mind off what's important. Think about it. How many times have you missed a turn, left your purse, lost your cell phone, or hurt yourself or someone else, because you were so aggravated?

The Bible says that Jesus will keep you in perfect peace, if you keep your mind on Him (Isaiah 26:3). But like I said, it's a choice. Chances are, if you are aggravated, your mind will be pulling you everywhere except Christ, and if you don't check it, aggravation will burn you out quickly.

Here are a couple of tips to keep aggravation from riding you. The Bible says love covers a multitude of sins.(1 Peter 4:8) Forgiveness people! Let the love of God rise up in you and enable you to push past the situation. Love that person! Secondly, don't say anything! James 1:19-20 reads, "You must all be quick to listen, slow to speak and slow to get angry."

Wait until you've had an opportunity to pray on the matter. That way you won't sin in your irritation. And last but not least, keep your eyes on God! He will rescue you from these traps (Psalm 25:15).

My friend, don't look to the right, nor to the left; keep your gaze forward on Jesus! Keep praying, and keep positive words coming out of lips. You don't have to stay aggravated. Choose to stay focused.

Notes_____

_____

_____

_____

_____

_____

_____

_____

_____

_____

_____

_____

_____

_____

_____

_____

_____

_____

_____

_____

_____

From Jealous to Zealous

When we look at someone else's blessing, and we think in our hearts, "Now how did they get that? I deserve that!" We plug up our pipe for purpose and blessing – like the nasty gunk that plugs up the drain in bathroom sinks. Yes, it's that gross. Whether it is covetousness, jealousy or envy, it's gross in the eyes of God, and we shouldn't touch it.

Coveting: lustful desire after something that belongs to someone else. A car, job, spouse, friendship, or even a person's body or looks – what God has for you is for you, in His timing. And what He doesn't have for you, you certainly don't want. It will fit irregularly into your life – causing rips, tears, kinks, and a busted heart.

Jealousy: the feeling that something that belongs to you is given to another person or object. Anger is cruel, and wrath is like a flood, but jealousy is even more dangerous (Proverbs 27:4). Red flags go up when the focus on a person is directed somewhere else. Thoughts of rejection and hurt can brew in your mind. You can overcome jealousy by knowing that God is always paying attention to you. He wants to be first-in-line for your attention all the time. Don't be afraid of change; God is still in control. Walk in love – love has no jealousy in it.

Last but not least, envy: like coveting and jealousy, but it involves a hatred for the person as well.

Don't envy violent people nor covet their ways (Proverbs 3:32). The Bible speaks about envying evil people often. But, don't envy your brother and sisters in Christ either. Hatred growing in your heart will sap your strength and keep you up late at night. Pray for the person you envy, and be a blessing to them.

Get zealous! Go after God and what He has for you with great eagerness and excitement. Seek God, and you will find Him, and you'll soon be asking yourself, "When did I turn from jealous to zealous?"

Notes_____

_____
_____
_____
_____
_____
_____
_____
_____
_____
_____
_____
_____
_____
_____
_____
_____
_____
_____

Poems for Inspiration and Revelation

Chasing After God

I chased after God this morning
No, he wasn't hiding
He was luring me into his presence
As I ran, He drew me deeper in His courts, never
going further than I could reach
He said, "Come daughter."
His voice pulled on my hearts strings
And anticipating His embrace
I ran swifter and faster
My strides got longer and my pores perspired
The joy of the Lord filled my lungs as I Inhaled
Exhaled smoothly.
I reached out
I was so close I could smell His essence
Smelled Holy and pure like how it does after it rains
And just, as our fingers almost touched
My spirit grew weak in my well doing
My flesh said, "No! Don't push me this far!"
My feet started to drag
And sweat ran into my eyes
And I could barely see Him there
He called my name
But I barely heard Him because my mind told me He
wasn't really there
You're almost there! He cried
My heart raced as it pounded against my ribs
But I just kept running
And I just kept reaching
And I never stopped
And I just kept believing
And I never stopped

And when my sight was at it's worst,
I squeezed my eyes shut and ran right into Him!
He grabbed hold of me so tightly
And I pressed my face against His and sighed, "I'll
never leave you again."
He wiped the sweat from my brow and tenderly
kissed my cheek and his breath breezed through my
hair
His words filled me with all the life I lost a long the
way
He spoke, I AM wherever you are
Seek and you will find me If you endure you'll find
I AM always near.
I AM never far.

Healed Me

When He healed me
When GOD HEALED ME
I can remember that day so vividly
I felt like a flower opening up to the sun
I danced and I spun
And my petals reached out for Him
His healing virtue hit my skin like rays from the sun
Soaked deep to my core, to my soul
And washed away all the bitter times
And then He said I'm healing your spine
So that you can stand and hold your head up
Healing passed clean through my bones like fire
He said I'm strengthening where you're tired
And then He healed my heart
He said every time your heart beats
I'm beating down the walls of Jericho
And giving you back your land
And no woman or man will be able to conqueror you
And the He said I'm washing your feet
Because you belong to me
I'm healing the places you should not have gone
And they will work for your good even though you
were wrong
And then He breathed His breath into my spirit
Clearing residue and every piece of debri
That was placed in my path to hinder me
And He healed my hands to do His will
To reach out to others no matter how I feel
And I felt new. I felt free.
I couldn't remember the old me, where I had been.
But the places I'd go

—

And the things I'd do
Was all I could see
I remember that day when I felt God stand with me
I remember that day when God healed me.

What's Happening?

What does it really mean when we ask for
forgiveness
What does it really mean when we repent
And the blood washes away sins stench
And we go about our day
Still bound in our ways
Like a criminal with his hands behind his back
Or a quarterback that got sacked

What really happens in our hearts
Is it sticky with malice like black tar
Is it dark and hollow like the trunk of a car
Are you locked in an older model without that safety
latch
Kidnapped by your old ways
Are you abducted by a carnal mind

What's happening in our brains
Is it void of the spirit
Are the scriptures being sucked out by a dirt devil
Like every time a word starts to sink in
A 50 volt vacuum sucks it out again

What's happening to this body
Every time a wound starts to heal
The hand rips open the scab
And infection gets in
Like gossip in the church and sex in the choir,
And the mouth says one thing and the body does
another
So the lips say truth but the body says liar?

86

What's happening
What are we gonna do?
Not just me I mean you
I mean like are we gonna stand like we're stuck like
Lot's wife
Or we are gonna look back and not really try
Are we gonna get a new mind
Are we gonna burn the tar from our hearts
With Pentecostal flames
Are we gonna stop jumping each other like this some
checkers game
No more king me, queen me
Are we gonna stretch out our hand and stop being
lame
I just wonna know
What's happening

About The Author

Letia Hughes is an author of Christian Fiction and Non-fiction literature. She is also known as Christian recording artist Lady Flame. Letia has ministered at teen, back to school and church events. Letia Hughes grew up in Tallahassee, Florida where she still resides. She loves making music, reading and teaching.

www.LetiaHughes.com

HIGHLY FLAMMABLE!

www.ingramcontent.com/pod-product-compliance
Lightning Source LLC
Chambersburg PA
CBHW060359050426
42449CB00009B/1805